ROSE THERAPY

My Journey of Growing and Caring for Roses

D1519918

RON DANIELS

FOREWORD BY
JOHN WENDLER, NASHVILLE ROSE SOCIETY

ROSE THERAPY

My Journey of Growing and Caring for Roses

Copyright 2023 Ron Daniels

Published in Phoenix, Arizona by Emissary Publishing. Emissary is a business trade name of Ed's Voices, LLC.

Scripture quotations are from the NIV Bible (The Holy Bible, New International Version), copyright 1978 by Biblica Ministries, a nonprofit Bible and publishing ministry.

Table of Contents

The grass withers, and the flowers fade;
but the word of our God stands forever.

Isaiah 4:8

There are three things that will endure - Faith, Hope and Love;
and the greatest of these is Love.

1 Corinthians 13:13

Foreword

By John Wendler of the Nashville Rose Society

As I grew up, my parents subscribed to a number of publications, including Reader's Digest. I looked forward to its arrival every month because there were a number of sections I really enjoyed – "Word Power", "Laughter", "Quotable Quotes," and especially "My Most Unforgettable Character." It inspired me to learn how one person, often met though a chance encounter, could impact another person in meaningful and long lasting ways. Sometimes the "unforgettable character" was famous; other times, it would be someone unassuming - you wouldn't consider them "special" on the surface.

Over the course of my business career, I've been fortunate to meet a number of famous people – former President Bill Clinton; professional athletes like Michael Jordan, Roger Clemens and Greg Norman; musicians like the band Alabama and Shania Twain, and a handful of billionaire businessmen. As thrilling as it was to meet "celebrities," none of them had any impact on my life beyond the meeting itself. Conversely, I've come across a few "unforgettable characters" who affected my life in a meaningful way. They were usually teachers who mentored me in school, pushing me to reach my personal, academic, and athletic potential. Never did I envision that, in my late sixties, I'd encounter another unforgettable character. But I did. His name is Ron Daniels.

I first met Ron in the fall of 2015. I'd started growing roses a few years earlier – without much success – and decided to join the Nashville Rose Society in a last-ditch effort to figure out my errors. I only had a few roses at the time, but I felt that if the Nashville Rose Society couldn't help me, I would throw in the towel and find a new hobby. So, I began attending NRS meetings every month. At the time, Ron was Vice President of Education for NRS. He showed great interest in my measly 4 roses, and how I cared for them (or failed to care for them) – and I liked him immediately. It's hard not to like him – he's very outgoing and gregarious, and his personality is infectious. He's one of the most genuine "people persons" I've ever met. It may sound like a cliché to say that he's probably never met anyone he didn't like, but I believe that to be true. Before long, Ron offered to mentor me, which started a journey and relationship that has only deepened since.

The more time Ron and I spent together, the more I learned how to grow healthy roses. I also learned a lot about *him*. For Ron, growing roses (and gardening in general) are much more than hobbies – they're ways of life, and a reflection of his journey. He came from very humble beginnings, and ascended to become the head of his own successful construction company, Custom Recreation. Likewise, his journey with roses started with 3 plants he purchased at K-Mart over 30 years ago. From being tutored and encouraged by his own mentor, John Curtis, that number grew to over 250 roses at one point.

Ron also says growing roses is a form of therapy for him. I find them therapeutic as well, but for Ron, they mean even more: he enjoys sharing his garden and roses with others, to bring pleasure to their lives. He cuts roses for members of his church who lose their loved ones. He makes rose arrangements for engaged couples in his church who can't afford flowers for their wedding ceremony. He opens his garden up to the public every spring and fall for tours, and attracts as many as 150 people from all over the country. Above all else, roses give Ron the opportunity to answer his true calling in life: a teacher and mentor. That's Ron Daniels – selfless, humble, putting others before himself, and never forgetting or straying far from his roots.

When Ron became President of the Nashville Rose Society, he asked me to replace him as Vice President of Education. At the end of his two-year term, we became Co-Presidents of NRS, positions we held simultaneously for three years. Our relationship grew - from teacher/student, to co-leaders, to life-long friends. Along the way, my journey with roses mirrored his – from an inauspicious start with just 4 measly roses, to over 70 roses in my garden. Thanks to Ron's mentorship, I have a beautiful, thriving garden, and I've even won some awards at local rose shows.

If you read this book, you'll learn the basics of growing and caring for roses. But hopefully, you'll also gain an appreciation for the ways roses can impact human lives. They've certainly affected my life for the better – as has Ron Daniels, "my most unforgettable character."

- John Wendler

rosarian (n.)

A person who loves and cultivates roses.

Part One

Chapter One –

A Brief History of Roses

"Though an old man, I am but a young gardener." - *President Thomas Jefferson*

For me, roses are far more than a simple flower. They've become a huge part of who I am, and why I do what I do. In the pages that follow, it's my privilege to share my story, as well as three decades of experience growing and caring for them. Roses are more than just a *hobby*; they're also a passion, a form of ministry, and an art. An art that takes time, practice, attentiveness and willingness to go through trial and error. For me, that's a good place to start.

Roses have a rich history, which makes building and maintaining a rose garden a unique experience. Our Founding Fathers cherished them in hardscape gardens, which were common features in antebellum homes. President George Washington grew them, and named one of them after his mother. Many of these gardens were created in the period before the American Civil War (1861-1865). They were designed in a formal style with geometric shapes, straight lines, and symmetrical plantings. They included paving stones, bricks, raised beds, pathways, patios and other outdoor surfaces for a clear route through the garden. In 1986, President Ronald Reagan proclaimed the rose as the national flower and floral emblem of the United States.

I once had the opportunity to help plan the restoration of the hardscape at Belle Air Mansion. Originally built in 1745 by Governor Samuel Ogle, the mansion played a significant role in the development of the state, as well as the country. Belle was home to a number of influential figures, and it doubled as a hospital during the Civil War! It was slated for destruction, to build a new set of condos. But a fellow by the name of Louis James purchased the property and rescued it. He and his wife restored the inside of the mansion. It took them two years, but they did wonderful work.

When the time came to restore the garden, Louis contacted the Nashville Rose Society. I was very excited!

Along with two other rosarians (a name for people who love and cultivate roses) from the Nashville Rose Society, we walked the entire property. We wanted to see what it would take to restore the rose garden. Louis hoped that with our expertise, we could draw up a plan of action he could execute for a full restoration.

The garden was overgrown with weeds. They pulled at my boots as we walked through. I was relieved to find much of the hardscape still intact. As I leaned down to study the plants, I found they had some sprouts coming up from the original roses among the weeds! Who knows what historic conversations took place in these gardens, or which political figures walked and talked here!

We could not hand Louis a simple plan. This project had a hefty scope, if he wanted to do it right. The weeds needed clearing, the soil needed amending, and the pH levels needed adjustment. They would likely need a mason to come out to work on the stones, and replace several of them. To my surprise, Louis didn't bat an eye. He smiled, thanked us for our good work, and proceeded to do everything we recommended.

When the work was finished, the difference blew me away. You can see the original bricks used in the hardscaping. All the weeds were cleared and removed. The soil was worked and prepped for roses, and they implemented the planting design right away. The finished result is a masterpiece brought back to life.

Projects like this fill my soul. They give me a chance to dive into the history of a rose garden. I enjoy discovering who used the garden, what roses they picked, and—if I'm lucky—why they picked them.

The Belle Air Mansion before we restored the hardscape, January 2020

Belle Aire after we discovered and restored the hardscape

Another eye-catching project we worked on was the Belmont Mansion. The Acklen family built it as a summer home between 1849 and 1853. They installed a heaven scent rose garden, with somewhere between 800-1000 roses. Together with the Nashville Rose Society, we had the opportunity to cultivate a small section of the land, with about 200 roses. As the work progressed, I felt it needed something more. I wasn't sure why —until I realized that all of the roses we grew in the garden were *modern roses*. Which (sadly) meant that none of them represented the original varieties in the Acklen hardstone garden!

I walked the Belmont University campus with Judy Fisher, the wife of the president. I said, "You know, there's nothing in the garden that Adelicia Acklen grew herself. Every rose that's in there is modern." We discussed a full restoration with the original rose species. I told her about all the roses Adelicia had in her garden, and how they were breeds we could still get. I even knew of a guy in Florida whose roses dated back to the 15th century! She grinned, gave me a plot of land, and green-lit restoration of the *original* Acklen rose garden.

My first stop was to a historian at Belmont University. When I told him of my plans, he set about digging until he found a small, yellowed paper. It was an actual nursery list from when they ordered roses in the 1860s. *I couldn't believe my eyes!* This little paper named several rose species we could get today!

But the excitement didn't stop there. We found this list was shared with the Hermitage, the historical home of President Andrew Jackson, 7th President of the United States. His rose garden was known to be magnificent. Both he and his wife took pride in it. Jackson even had his wife buried in this garden, her tomb surrounded by beautiful thriving roses.

This evidence showed that the Hermitage and the Belmont Mansion shared rose orders together! With this research, I found 50% of the roses Adelicia actually grew at the Belmont. We put about 20 roses in the garden and labeled it the "Adelicia Acklen Rose Garden." Today, it's a thriving beauty.

(The Belmont rose gardens are maintained by the great Belmont landscaping team.)

The statue of Faith (as in, "Faith, Hope and Love") outside the original Belmont Mansion

Roses are the most important plant in a Southern garden. They were planted in nearly every antebellum home. Even Thomas Jefferson grew roses! But roses aren't just in our background. They show up in *everybody's* history.

Fossil evidence suggests roses have a long evolutionary history dating back millions of years. One of the oldest known fossilized roses is a species called Rosa Eocenica, which was found in Montana and is estimated to be 35 million years old! The cultural and historical significance of roses can't be overstated, if you ask me. They've been admired for millennia, and played roles in art, literature, mythology, and passion.

Ancient Greek, Roman, and Egyptian civilizations grew roses, and made numerous uses of their benefits. They grew them for decorating, celebrating, mourning, healing, cooking and worshiping. They found them useful for aromatic purposes, such as early perfumes and oils. And they continue to serve those same purposes today.

It's hard to overstate the economic value of roses. We grow them for bouquet arrangements, perfumes, oils, flavoring, and other consumer goods. With unique taste and potent aroma, rose flavored drinks, ice creams, and candies are common and popular. The floral flavor is light and sweet, enhancing many dishes. The rose industry is a big part of the global economy. In addition to their usefulness, roses offer environmental benefits. With over 150 species and thousands of cultivars, they boost the ecosystem and attract pollinators such as bees, butterflies, and hummingbirds.

Roses are beautiful, valuable and useful, and they're also *important*. They are powerful illustrations of how God infuses beauty into our world, sparking the passion of rosarians like me. If you want to become a rosarian, I suggest you look for the deeper meaning in the roses you grow. Find a species that "speaks" to you, both in history and beauty. In today's world, we can find the roses that mean something to us personally, and plant them in our gardens. The connection you form to the roses you grow is what makes it a fulfilling hobby.

Chapter Two –

Common Problems Growing and Caring for Roses

The only difference between you (as a novice) and a master rosarian is your degree of knowledge. Other than that, you have (or can access) everything you need to master this art.

Roses have a reputation as "finicky" plants (though modern varieties are more hardy), which makes them a little scary for novice rosarians. The best way to gain experience with growing them is through focusing on the basics, and there are several mistakes likely to happen - no matter which species you choose. I've seen people pick up the hobby of roses, only to put it back down quickly because they didn't get it right the first time. That's the wrong attitude if you want to work with roses!

Here are some common issues, and how to avoid them:

1. Incorrect Soil

To successfully grow roses, you have to get your hands dirty. You'd be surprised how many people tell me they bought a bag of Holy Cow Soils (a fantastic organic garden soil I recommend), and then all they did was add it on top of their dirt! That's a good start, but it only helps so much if your roses are planted in clay. You can't sprinkle soil on, the way you would with fertilizer; it needs to be mixed in <u>deep</u>. Which means you have to get your hands dirty.

Don't forget - you'll have to <u>amend</u> your soil to get the best results. Amending creates the nutrients required to improve structure and fertility. It also improves drainage with sand, increases fertility with specific compost and fertilizers, adjusts the pH, and improves the structure with organic matter or manure. There's no such thing as "magic fertile soil" … but there is a formula. If you do A, B, and C, in other words, you'll get quality soil for roses.

In my own garden I have 28 inches of amended soil. Here is the formula I recommend:

- ⅓ top soil (Holy Cow Soil)

- ⅓ sand

- ⅓ organic materials (plant or animal matter)

- Sandy loam soil (roses love it!)

In addition, measure your pH levels. You may need to add limestone or sulfur to adjust. pH is a measure of how acidic or basic a substance is. "pH" stands for "potential hydrogen," and it's how you measure the concentration of hydrogen ions in a solution. A solution with a high concentration of hydrogen ions is considered **acidic**, while a solution with a low concentration of hydrogen ions is considered **basic**, or alkaline.

The pH scale ranges from zero to 14, with 7 being neutral. Anything below 7 is considered acidic, and anything above 7 is considered basic. For example, a solution with a pH of 4 is more acidic than a solution with a pH of 5, and a solution with a pH of 9 is more basic than a solution with a pH of 8. When cultivating roses, you want a measurement of 6.0-6.5 on the pH scale in your soil. If your acidity is too low, use Dolomitic Garden Lime, or Limestone F to improve it. And if the pH is too high, use sulfur.

pH is important because it can affect the growth and health of plants. Different plants have different pH preferences. Your soil's pH must match the plant's needs to create a growth environment for your roses. If you don't measure the pH of your soil, your garden will struggle.

This may sound complicated, but don't worry! Even I had trouble with the pH levels in my garden at first. My mentor, John Curtis, helped me pick out Double Delight, Mister Lincoln, and Peace roses. The first year they bloomed wonderfully, but the second year, they didn't bloom well. I reacted the same way many novice rosarians do - I got frustrated. I didn't know what I had done wrong, and it felt like I had failed as a rosarian.

John came over with a pH meter and took a reading of my soil. This immediately showed me the problem: *the pH was in the 5.0 range!* He chuckled and advised me on which limestone to purchase, and how much to add so my roses would start growing again. Needless to say, I was happy someone knew what they were doing! Once I followed John's instructions, my roses came back to life again.

Fixing your pH levels takes time, and that is *okay*. Give yourself grace in this process. As you manage your soil year to year, keep in mind you will need to do ongoing maintenance and restoration to help maintain the soil nutrients. It's like changing the oil on your car; you can't do just one round and assume it's "fixed" forever. In the spring, when the ground thaws, you'll need to check your soil again and replace nutrients so your roses can thrive in the new year.

Use lime to increase your soil's pH, and sulfur (left) to decrease it

A pH meter measures the acidity and alkalinity of the soil

2. Growing On The North Side of the House

One time, a woman came to our workshop eager to learn about growing and maintaining a rose garden. She participated in the workshop with an excited smile and a curious heart. Armed with all the knowledge we could give her, she eagerly began cultivating her own roses. But she didn't get the results she hoped for—and came back upset.

When she shared her disappointment, I offered to visit her garden to find a solution. I brought a pH meter. The soil was decent, but I noticed a different problem when she showed me where she'd planted the roses. They were on the <u>north</u> side of her house! This location, paired with soil that was decent but didn't have good pH levels, led to poor growth. We helped her move her garden, and today she's an avid member of our society who grows a lot of roses!

Few novice rosarians consider location when they plant their roses. Is it the *right* location? This is a big part of the success of any garden. Just like with real estate, you have to think: "Location, location, location!" Roses need plenty of sunlight to thrive. Aim for a location that gets close to six or more hours of direct sunlight per day. The best locations usually face east, south or west.

Once you settle on the best location, I would encourage you to consider building raised beds for your roses. Getting down on your knees to access a plant is troublesome for anyone, especially as you get older. But this is about more than knee and back pain; raised beds are also prime for drainage control. They make it easier to maintain the roses themselves. I would recommend somewhere between 18 inches wide and up to 28 inches deep.

3. Roses Don't Like Wet Feet

Unfortunately, it's easy to both over-water and under-water your roses.

Roses need a good drink of water, but they don't like to sit in wet soil. This can give them "root rot." It's a delicate balance that takes time and patience to get right. Before you water, check the soil. Is it wet? If so, skip the watering. Is it dry? Go ahead and water.

Aim for two inches of water per week, either from rain or irrigation. But remember - the amount of water your roses need can vary. It depends on the species of rose, the age of the plant, the weather, and the soil conditions. This is why you have to learn the names of your roses, and research what they need. Each rose thrives under different conditions.

Use a hose or a drip system with a timer (which you can automate) when you water, to give your roses a deep soak and encourage a strong root system. Apply a layer of mulch around your roses, to help retain the moisture in the soil and reduce the frequency of watering. **Don't overhead-spray your roses**. They don't like to be overhead-sprayed. In fact, if a novice rosarian tells me their roses have developed diseases, the first thing I ask them is whether they overhead-sprayed their roses.

A drip system with emitters ensures your plant's roots get watered evenly all around the base

I use ¼ inch in-line drip tubing. Look closely at the tiny holes punctured on the right, and you can see where water drips out

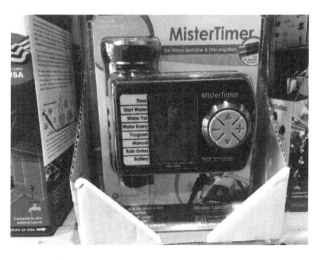

Timers are useful for creating rhythms and routines for your roses

Half-inch mainline pipes connect your timer to your in-line drip tubes

4. Not Pruning

John Curtis always told me, "There is no such thing as bad pruning unless it is *no pruning at all*."

As with watering, it's easy to prune too much, or too little. It's an elusive balance that takes experience to master. Many novice rosarians don't know exactly what they should prune, or where. They often turn to a "hack and saw" method that leads to oddly shaped bushes and poor growth. This is a skill you have to practice.

Rose pruning keeps your roses healthy and looking their best. It involves removing dead, diseased, or damaged branches from the roses, as well as thinning out excess growth to promote the overall health and vigor of the plant.

To prune your roses, you'll need a pair of sharp pruning shears or loppers. Start by removing the "Three Ds" - *dead*, *diseased*, or *damaged* branches. These branches will be easy to spot, as they'll be dry, brittle, or otherwise unhealthy. Spring pruning is key to taming your roses as they come out of dormancy and begin to put on new growth.

Next, take a look at the overall shape of your rose bush. If it's looking a little overgrown or unruly, you can thin out some of the excess growth to promote better air circulation and sunlight penetration. Be sure to leave a few healthy canes on the plant, so it has a strong framework to support new growth. Remove any "suckers" (new stems growing from the base or roots of the plant as it tries to spread). Suckers drain energy from the plant, and removing them promotes better health. Any new growth coming from the bud union(location where rose is grafted on root stock) should not be removed.(This is called a basal break and will be a new cane to produce your roses.)

As your rose bushes continue through the season, you'll add dead-heading to your pruning ritual. "Dead-heading" is a term used to describe the process of removing spent flowers or cutting blooms from a plant. When a flower begins to fade or wilt, it's considered "spent." It's a good idea to remove it from the plant to encourage new growth and prevent the plant from putting energy into seed production.

When you find a spent flower, use your pruning shears to remove it by cutting the stem just above a five leaf of the flower. Be sure to cut the stem at a 45-degree angle to encourage new growth. Dead-heading helps keep your plants looking neat and tidy, and encourages the production of new flowers.

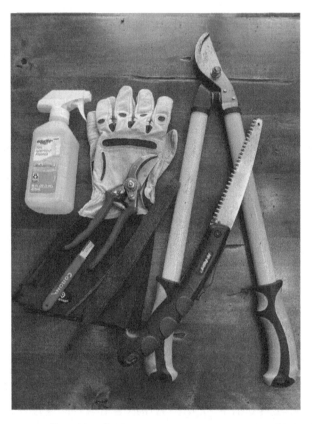

Gloves, loppers (yellow handles), pruning saw, pruners (red handles), file for sharpening and rubbing alcohol (to disinfect between bushes). Everything you need for pruning

A fully spring-pruned bush, after fertilization and with lime added after checking pH levels.

5. The Promise of a Rose Garden

Being a member of the Nashville Rose Society (NRS) for more than 20 years, I often wondered why we didn't have a rose garden onsite at Cheekwood Botanical Gardens.

Cheekwood Estate is where our NRS meetings are held. It's a semi-famous landmark in Nashville, Tennessee, and the former home and gardens of the Cheek family, founders of the Maxwell House Coffee brand. We've had our monthly meetings and rose shows there for many years, but we've never had a rose garden on the property. Not one!

So I made it my goal to find out if we could create a garden at Cheekwood. I felt we needed a beautiful rose garden to show

, especially during our NRS meetings. This way new members *and* the public could come to learn about ᴜnting and caring for roses with a "hands-on garden." As I researched, I found we *did* have a rose garden back in the early 1990s. I found out that it became too much for the NRS to maintain, so they had it removed.

Now that I knew there'd been a rose garden on the property at some point, my plans became a little easier. I shared my vision with NRS members. Together, we arranged a meeting with decision-makers at Cheekwood to talk about a possible "teaching" rose garden on the estate. Together with Sam Jones, our Tenarky District Director, and Todd Breyer, the Landscape Architect at Cheekwood, we came up with a plan to build the teaching garden.

As we talked it through, I could see them nodding with excitement. We walked the grounds together and Todd offered two possible areas we could use for the new rose garden. Once we got the green light, I started contacting vendors and friends of the NRS about donating materials to build the garden. Believe it or not, every person I called agreed to donate something toward the effort!

Our local society of NRS paid for the labor and miscellaneous expenses, while our members planted over 52 roses! We included all kinds, with some special requests from Cheekwood, including Hybrid Teas, Grandifloras, Miniatures,

Floribundas, Minifloras, Shrubs, Old Garden Roses (OGRs), Climbers,Earth Kind Roses and Rugosas.

And so the "Rose Study Garden in Partnership with Cheekwood" was born. Today, during our meetings, we spend part of the time in our garden, maintaining and learning from it together. It was worth every minute of hard work and planning, and has renewed our goal to share the love of roses with others. It's been unbelievable to see how it affected our membership, as well as the nearby community and visitors to Cheekwood.

This would never have happened if I hadn't asked the question, "Why don't we have a rose garden here?" Sometimes, the biggest problem that comes with growing roses is that people don't see the *promise* of growing them. That's totally fine, if you're not moved by them. But if you're reading this book, they probably matter to you. So you need to understand the promise that comes with learning to grow roses. More than just beauty, there are so many benefits to you as a person, as well as the people whose lives you touch by doing it.

People don't always think about roses as a way to connect with their community or enhance the relationships in their lives. Many disqualify themselves as "not talented enough," or they think they don't have a "green thumb." But what if it's not about that? What if, by merely having a rose garden of your own, you can develop your own character, and share the goodness you reap from the process? Many people start with zero plant knowledge. But by persevering, they become master rosarians with beautiful gardens who share and pass on their knowledge to others.

The Rose Study Garden at Cheekwood, just after completion in 2015

The orange tree added to the Rose Study Garden. Every fall, it takes five men to move it to the greenhouse for the winter!

The sign in the front of the Rose Study Garden that greets people when they enter. It took John Wendler four months to get it approved!

6. The Reasons for Your Roses

Why do you want to become a rosarian? What roses do you want to plant specifically? And the *big question...why* have you chosen *those* roses? If you know why you've started working with a particular rose or species, it's easier to keep going when things get difficult.

Now you might read this and think, *"Come on, Ron, they're just roses!"* But roses are demanding, laborious, and time-consuming. If you don't step into this world with a *"why"* fueling your passion, you're likely to give up the hobby quickly. I've seen it happen with too many quitters for it to be a string of coincidences.

So, take a step back and ask yourself, "Why?" That way the roses you pick will be meaningful to you. You'll know the history behind them. You'll know the names of your roses, which gives you in-depth knowledge about their care. Most people can't tell the quality of a plant from the box store versus one from the White House Rose Garden. What's more, they "don't know what they don't know" - to them, there *is* no difference between the two.

And there are so many roses to choose from! You can dive into Old Garden roses, which existed before 1867, or hybrid teas (most commonly associated with actress Marilyn Monroe). You can look for taller roses like Grandiflora, or tree roses. And miniature, miniflora roses, shrub roses, and climbing roses are great to position on the side of your home. There is even a groundcover rose!

The Marilyn Monroe is a hybrid tea that makes an excellent show rose

This hobby requires *passion*. The roses you pick should be ones you feel a connection with, so that you can't wait to get out into the garden.

7. Find A Mentor

We address and fix these common mistakes in my workshops and NRS meetings. They are also some of the first things a master rosarian will ask when you have problems in your garden. I urge you to seek help when you need it. You don't have to figure this out by yourself. You'll make connections with gardeners and rosarians who share your passion and love to help others learn.

My mentor, John Curtis, helped me pick out my first few roses and talked me through the pros and cons of each one. He helped me amend my soil, and talked through issues as they came up. He taught me the particulars of pruning, and how to prevent diseases. With John on my side, I knew I could become a great rosarian.

If you find yourself asking:

- What are the best varieties of roses to plant in my garden?
- How do I plant and care for roses?
- How do I protect my roses from pests and diseases?
- How often should I water, spray and fertilize my roses?

Then it's time to find an expert who can help.

I hate to see younger people try to learn how to grow roses from YouTube videos or Google searches. Those things are handy for basic information, but the truth is you need to work with someone who knows what they're doing. You need to get your hands in the soil! And no matter how much information you find in those videos, you'll go further with a mentor.

The learning never stops. I haven't learned everything there is to know about roses. It's a hobby for people with a growth mindset. There are always new things to learn, and tactics to try. Some will work for you and some won't—but as long as you have a willingness to experiment, you'll figure out which is which.

Rose societies across the world are ready and willing to help. These groups, like Nashville Rose Society (where I'm a member) are full of people with passion to help others experience the joy and love of growing roses. We conduct workshops and celebrate our roses together! Take the shortcut, and find yourself a mentor.

Part 2

Chapter Three –

My Rosy Past

I thought I'd share a little bit about my background and the importance of roses in my family.

You don't have to come from a family of gardeners to be a successful rosarian - but for me, it helped. Have you ever witnessed a family that excels at something together? Think of famous football families where the children, parents and grandparents all played in college or the NFL. I had the same thing with roses. I come from *three* generations of gardeners, and each one taught me valuable lessons about and maintaining a plot of land. From their influence and teachings, I learned to grow my own garden. It became a lifelong passion. I'm still doing it, over 30 years after I planted my first roses.

I don't know if I would have found my way to gardening without my family. Each one of them took me under their wing and showed me how to look at a garden through a new lens. That's the thing about gardening—there are so many different ways to do it. Skills and techniques evolve over time, as well as technology and resources. And because my family passed down such a passion for growing to me, I've had the pleasure of perfecting their lessons and paying them forward to others.

Family History

At age ten, I remember running through my grandmother's garden in a state of wonder. It seemed like she grew every plant you could imagine. Surrounded by a full orchard, a manicured garden, and blossoming roses, I was amazed. We visited her often, and every time I explored her gardens, I found something new.

I remember stretching out my hands and feeling the textures of different leaves. Rose petals felt like velvet, and orchard tree leaves felt leathery to the touch. I would walk for hours through the garden pathways, under the shade of the orchard trees, feeling the liveliness of the greenery around me. Different scents fought for my attention as I drifted through the rows and pathways. Her garden was like Neverland to me—a secret place the world would never find.

One Sunday afternoon, as I walked through the spiraling pathways, I discovered I wasn't alone. Several other people were meandering through her garden as well! I wondered where they'd come from, and why they were there. Later, I learned that she opened her garden to the community on a weekly basis. She connected with neighbors this way, and they also connected with her. People of every age and walk of life appreciated the beauty of her work.

Mam Maw Powell was one of the most passionate gardeners I knew as a kid. This soft-hearted woman continued gardening well into her eighties!

She would put her hand on my shoulder and point out different plants to me. I tried to remember their names. As we walked throughout the garden, she would stop to chat with people who came to visit. She wanted them to feel welcome (and informed, if they wanted to grow gardens of their own). Through her example, I learned how to share my garden and connect with others through it. No matter our differences, we can enjoy the beauty of plants as common ground.

I wasn't the only one my grandmother influenced. She taught my dad to become a gardener as well, especially after my grandfather passed away.

I remember helping my dad delicately pick weeds. As the oldest of my siblings, I was the first one to work in the garden. Since I gave Daddy the help he needed, my siblings soon found other interests, and never caught the gardening bug the way I did. The garden became a place where we connected. It was a safe place where we talked, laughed, and learned together. Daddy also had a deep well of knowledge about gardening that he passed on to me.

He taught me the difference between a sprout of a plant—the kind you want to keep—and the sprout of a weed. Together we cultivated a perennial garden, and a vegetable garden. He didn't grow many roses, but he loved perennials. I've got a lot of good memories from digging our hands in the dirt and passing time together under the sun. Daddy was very attuned to nature. I think he learned it from living in a rural area.

When we watered, I learned about the maintenance schedules of zucchini and corn. He showed me exactly how much water each crop needed, and how to tell if they were overwatered. When pulling weeds, he'd talk about planting depth and pruning for perennial plants. When we rolled the soil between our fingers, he described to me what "good" soil felt like, versus soil that needed its nutrients replaced. And just like my grandmother, Daddy always shared his crops and plants with the community and our family.

As we worked together, his passion became my passion. I could always retreat to the garden to forget about the cares of the world. When I had trouble in school, the garden soothed my frustration. As I grew into a young man full of hormones I couldn't quite cope with, the garden gave me an escape. It was a place where the only thing I had to worry about was a bunch of little green sprouts and the signals they gave us for their needs.

Gardening also showed up on Mama's side of the family as well. My maternal grandparents lived on a farm. For them, gardening served as more than a hobby; it was a way of life. They did what's called "survival gardening." They fed themselves with the fruits and vegetables they grew, and rarely bought produce from the store.

My grandfather on Mama's side was the best vegetable grower I knew. His tomatoes and corn were mouthwatering! He had a natural talent. Whenever he talked about how to grow things, I listened with a keen ear.

My family deeply influenced my gardening passion. They were the catalysts for me to start my own garden, when I grew up and owned my own land. I always kept a vegetable garden and some flowers throughout my twenties and thirties, and used the knowledge my family passed down to help it thrive. They taught me that to grow anything worthwhile takes desire and commitment.

I helped my father and grandfather plant and maintain the last gardens they kept before they passed away. Granddaddy died when I was 15 years old, shortly after the growing season ended; Daddy passed away in 1999 when I was fifty, also at the end of the growing season.

To this day, I still enjoy working on and cultivating my passion. I find great pleasure and significance in helping others learn and enjoy gardening. I believe in mentoring, and I *love* sharing and teaching in my garden. It's pure joy watching others learn what they can achieve with a little bit of hard work and dedication.

Construction

I enjoyed a long and prosperous career in the construction industry. I founded a company called Custom Recreation, which develops playgrounds, recreation areas, parks, and green ways. For many years I owned and operated the business, and taught my son how to run it. Today, he's in charge of the entire operation, and I have the privilege of helping and advising him.

Construction taught me a lot about gardening, oddly enough. We have a saying in construction: "What one man does affects the next man." It's a way of saying that whatever you do on this job will affect the workers who come after you. The best construction workers think ahead, and do the job right so that each phase of the project gets completed in the right way.

Multiple generations have the same effect on each other through gardens. As a third generation gardener, I now teach people how to grow their own gardens. But what they learn from me is (mostly) what I learned from my parents and grandparents. There's only so much you can do with plants, soil, water and sunlight. But with *people*? There's no telling what you can "grow" in another person, if you get the mixture right.

In construction, if we did our job right the first time, we could finish projects ahead of schedule, stay under budget, and move on to the next project. But with roses and people, there's no way to predict or calculate the goodness you can find.

When I ran my business, gardening helped me relieve stress. I'd come home from work and walk through my garden first, instead of going straight to the front door. Being among the blooms allowed me to calm down, before I saw my family. I didn't want to walk in and unload stress on my wife and children. If you're an entrepreneur, you know what I mean when I say that you're *never* "off the clock." Most of the time, construction is a stressful working environment. There are deadlines, heavy lifting, lots of logistics, and juggling of resources. It's draining.

But in my garden, those issues faded away. I enjoyed the sweet scents of my flowers and vegetables. I saw them thrive, and it restored calm and balance before I stepped through the doorway into my home.

Another lesson I learned through construction was the ability to persevere, even when difficulties came up. Business requires you to stay the course. If I had a problem, I kept working at it until I solved it. I didn't always make the smartest decisions in business, but I knew this: *nobody* could outwork me.

My son, who experienced a difficult phase because of COVID-19, once asked me, "Dad, how did you get through the hard times? You didn't just give up, even though things were tough in the 80s. What did you do?"

I said, "I'm a firm believer you can gain from anything you go through that has adversity attached to it." There were low points, and if I gave in, they had the power to drag me down into the mud. But I remembered that if you work hard, at some level, you will get results.

It was no different in my garden. Even when my plants struggled and I wasn't sure how to help them, I pushed through. I did research and tried new techniques until I got the results I wanted. Many gardeners have to work their way to success through trial and error. It doesn't come just because you plant seeds. It's a labor of love, and labors of love take time. But I can tell you this: it's worth it.

The construction business also boosted my gardening knowledge. I understand grades, which are important in construction because the slope of the land affects the stability and safety of a structure. It turns out, they also affect roses. I understand drainage, or how water flows on a specific piece of land - which also affects roses. I'm handy at creating "borders," to naturally separate earth, rock, hardscapes, beds, flowers, and trees. These influence the growth of roses. Occasionally, we got contracts where we planted trees and shrubs as well, giving me plenty of practice.

Construction taught me to understand the importance of site conditions and apply the same logic to gardening.

Today, I can observe an environment and tell whether or not it's good for growing roses. Some rosarians don't understand what I mean when I ask, "What are your site conditions?" It's how I assess the land, determining whether it needs adjustment for planting. I can tell how someone's house is suitable for growing by the grade, the drainage, the rock underneath the soil, how the area is currently shaped, how much soil is needed, and the locations that are available. It's a gift I've used to help others find the best places and conditions for their own rose gardens.

K-Mart Roses

I remember when I decided to start growing roses. It came unexpectedly—I saw rose bushes for sale in a K-Mart one day, and decided to buy three of them. Afterward, I felt a little buyer's remorse; my knowledge of roses was severely limited. Knowing I'd got myself in a pickle, I confessed my worries to a friend in a local restaurant. Somehow, I felt like *my* roses would be nothing compared to the ones my grandmother grew.

Seated just a few tables away was John Curtis, the man who would become my mentor. He overheard us talking, and walked over to introduce himself. He smiled, shook my hand and said, "Son, are you trying to grow roses?"

I said, "The keyword is 'trying.' I just got three, and I'm struggling."

"Well, if you've got a few minutes after you eat, I live about a mile from here. I want you to come see my rose garden."

Although I had just met John, I knew I could trust him. Have you ever met someone like that? I needed all the help I could get, so I figured, "Why not?"

I should have braced myself. As soon as I stepped into his rose garden, with over 600 roses, I couldn't find the words to speak. It blew me away! I realized I was in the presence of a master. John had grown roses for over 40 years!

We walked through his rose garden together, the sun shining down on us and the air filled with a sweet rosy perfume. I couldn't help but stop and admire the different colors and shapes of the blooms. It was enchanting.

John walked along quietly beside me, naming the different roses as I studied them. He pointed out drip water systems and soils he adjusted for different species of rose. I can't remember how long we walked together like this, but I recall that day with a deep sense of nostalgia. I hadn't walked through a rose garden like this since my grandmother passed away. And suddenly I wanted—I *needed*—to build something like it as well.

John must have seen the passion in my eyes because he smiled and said, "Would you like me to show you how to build a garden like this one?"

"Yes," I replied.

So, we built my first garden together. John came over, looked at the K-Mart roses, and helped me find the perfect location for them. Once we found it, he talked to me about the soil. Step by step, he helped me prep the ground for their planting. Afterwards we sat down together over a glass of sweet tea and designed a plan for care and fertilization. And when they weren't growing as well as I expected, John helped me figure out why—and adjust the pH levels of my soil. He mentored me for the next three years.

Mr. Curtis in his rose garden, captured by The Tennessean in the late 1980s

Chapter Four –

Stop and Smell the Roses

Once I planted those first bushes in the soil, I fell in love with roses.

Caring for and maintaining them felt "new" in one way, and familiar in another. From all the time I'd spent in my own garden, and those of people I loved, I recognized the familiar rituals of planting. But growing my own roses was a new kind of adventure. It wasn't long before those three rose bushes turned into six, then twelve, and so on. Soon, much of the planting area around our house became my first official rose garden.

These years were filled with learning seminars, long afternoons with John, connections with other rosarians, and joining the rose society. There were a lot of steps between then and now, but John walked with me through each one.

My Mentor

The more I got to know John Curtis, the more I admired him. Shannon Lane, a friend who went to college with my wife, knew John and sang his praises. "He's one of the best around!" she said. "If he has offered to mentor you, you get yourself a yellow pad and follow him around like a puppy dog, because he is going to teach you some stuff!"

So that's what I did.

For the next three years I wrote down everything John taught me. He was a gentle man, the kind you want to be around when you're learning something. His deep well of patience never ran out. His explanations were calm and clear. And no matter how many times you forgot something, he was always happy to explain it again. He had what I think God wants all of us to have for each other - "the heart of a teacher." Anytime you visited John's rose garden, he would offer you a piece of his famous lemon ice box pie.

After planting those first three roses, John and I went on to plant another 20 rose bushes together in my personal rose garden. His style of gardening worked well with mine. He used similar methods that I learned while growing vegetables. As my rose garden grew, so did the maintenance schedule - so John helped me outline and track it. Together, we set up a drip water system and I learned the secrets of pruning.

One day, while we amended the soil for a new rose bush, John told me about his family. His wife had passed away after 15 years of terminal illness. The rose garden was therapeutic, amid the challenge of caring for her. Those long nights and struggling days were difficult, but he could always find solace in his garden. His daughter had grown up and moved out, and unfortunately, she was not interested in gardening. He couldn't pass his knowledge along to her - which is why he was eager to help others (like me) learn to do it. Sharing the knowledge he developed was one of the ways he remained active and generous, late into his life.

John took me to the Nashville Rose Society and introduced me to several people he knew. I remember feeling intimidated, at first. I wasn't yet a member, but they made sure I felt welcome and comfortable. Many in the society nicknamed John "The Rose Man" and "The Rose Farmer," because his methods resembled growing vegetables. He showed roses at several competitions and taught workshops. People looked to him to learn. Once I got comfortable, the society itself became like a second family to me.

John taught me even more about life than he did about roses. The roses were simply a way to break the ice and meet people. The real magic happens when one human being connects with another. He used to say, "Promise that you'll share your garden, your knowledge and your flowers with somebody. Go bless someone who's hurting, had a loss, or celebrating." John believed that growing flowers helps us stay active in the lives of others, and show them we care. I learned how to relate to people better through John. He was magnetic; everyone wanted to be around him. When he gave someone a rose or shared his knowledge, it comforted them. The effect he had on people was profound.

And John didn't want his knowledge of rose growing techniques to be forgotten, or locked away. He believed in teaching. Because of him, I continue to teach everywhere I can. Whether at workshops, conferences, garden clubs, among master gardeners and rose societies, or engaging people one-on-one. Each time I teach them a new technique, I tell them what John told me:

"Make sure you share this with someone else!"

Before John died, he gave me several of the roses in his garden as gifts, which I cherished. To this day, I can name the rose bushes he gave me, which now grow in my own garden. I even have a sign posted as the "John Curtis Miniature Rose Garden"! It's a small reminder of the power roses have to connect people. I'm grateful for the time I had with John. He set me on the path to becoming a master rosarian. From following his example, I've learned to help others on their own journeys with roses.

The sign that sits in my garden to this day, reminding me of John Curtis and the impact he had on my life through growing roses

The Effect of Roses On My Soul

As my ability to grow and maintain roses developed, I also cultivated a new mindset towards the people around me: grace.

John said, "Always show grace. You never know what condition someone is in."

I didn't understand what that had to do with roses at the time, but today I know it well. Roses are more than just pretty flowers; they lift our souls and improve our lives. Anytime he was on the street, or he went to someone's house, John always took roses with him to give away. And though he could have found plenty of reasons to be unhappy, he never did. Helping others find joy was his passion.

Through John's example, I became better at showing grace to people, even if they were hurting, unhappy, or upset. In the construction business, everyone points fingers when things go wrong. People get angry, they raise their voices, and exchange heated words. I later realized that one reason our company was so successful came from my commitment to imitate John's example in the workplace. It took time, but we learned to *avoid* pointing fingers, raising voices or assuming the worst about people. (If I could have got my employees to start growing their own rose gardens, I would have done it!)

When I talk to people about roses, they immediately recall their own stories: pinning a rose on their blouse on Easter Sunday, or the memory of roses grown by a departed loved one. There is always a certain depth behind roses, and it doesn't take long to find it. Sometimes, it's the memory of a rose itself; I can tell by the excitement in a person's eyes.

As my garden grew, others took more interest. It seemed to elevate their attitudes and help them relax. I opened up my garden so visitors could come and experience it, just like I'd seen my grandmother do. When children come to the garden, I always give them a rose to take home. The oldest visitor in my garden was a lady at the age of ninety-nine. She didn't just walk into my garden … she *ran* into it with excitement! She got a few roses from me as well. One time, a guy I hadn't seen for 40 years stopped into my garden to say hello!

Some of the youngest visitors to my garden. Every year, I cut them a different rose and encourage them to remember the names

I've heard several people say, "I feel like the roses are hugging me." That makes me smile. Early in life, I struggled to empathize with people who were different from me. But John's influence helped me grow, so that today I can connect with anyone I talk to. These days, I'm more curious than I used to be about people's sorrows, losses and pain. I'm creative in how I do things and treat people. I'm slow to judge. I get to *share* (instead of boast) about what I have. I'm a kinder, gentler version of myself - because of growing roses.

In the difficult days of the COVID pandemic, I gathered and gave away dozens of roses to nurses at a local hospital

The Effect of Roses On My Mind

I'm also more experienced at avoiding the problems we covered in Part One. As I kept showing up at the Rose Society, I began to teach workshops. Several people came to hear what I had to say. To my surprise, I was quickly asked to come speak to larger groups. If you'd have told me that one day, I'd speak publicly to groups of as many as 200 people at a time, I'd have laughed. But that's exactly what I do! I've done it so many times, I don't even get nervous anymore. I'm eager to get up on a stage and share my passion. At speaking engagements, I will stand at the front door and greet people as they enter. Then I get up and tell my story. I know the subject matter like the back of my hand.

Now I'm a ARS Master Consulting Rosarian with the American Rose Society. I've been elected the President of the Nashville Rose Society. I've won the ARS Glenda Whitaker Award, a Bronze Honor Medal, I serve as a consulting rosarian for Belmont University, and a Master Gardener for Summer Country Master Gardeners in the state of Tennessee! That shows you how far one person can go, if you take the time to teach them, like John Curtis did for me.

One of the regular meetings of the Nashville Rose Society

Turning Towards Ministry

Growing and sharing roses with others became my personal mission. An old Persian proverb says, "The world is a rose; smell it, and pass it to your friends."

Because of the deep connections roses create, you'll find many ways you can minister with them. Teaching is a form of ministry for me. The reactions on the faces of people I teach are like the eyes of a kid staring at Christmas lights. My workshops are a positive, no-stress zone; people drive from as far away as 100 miles to visit my rose garden. I personally greet everyone who comes. Once, I had an entire neighborhood association ask me to visit and speak to them!

Another thing I love is when people call, email or text after a presentation to say, "After listening to you, I'm going to try growing my own roses!" That fires me up. It's how I know the joy has spread. When attendees find success, they will often create their first bouquet and send me a picture of it. I love all the feedback and progress people share!

However, ministering with roses goes much deeper than teaching. At a more profound level, they can become powerful gifts during important moments in people's lives. Few things have brought me more joy and comfort than in comforting others with roses.

The first time I saw this was when John Curtis asked me to help him bring flowers every week to the women's ministry at his church. They would distribute them to the sick and the shut-in, or to people who simply needed encouragement. I saw the effect of it firsthand. The roses made lasting impressions.

After John passed away, I started a similar version at Long Hollow Baptist Church, where I attend services. I had never done anything like this, but I knew how much happiness it brought John, so I decided to give it a try, and see if God would add His blessing. In those days, we focused on widows, so they could have roses on their birthdays or anniversaries. I would prepare the bouquets, take them to church, and the women's ministry would distribute them.

This ministry didn't stay small for long! Soon, I found myself preparing roses year-round, on request. Even in the wintertime, when I didn't have roses in my own garden, I purchased them from a friend in the business (who charged me only a few pennies for them) so people with birthdays in winter could still have a bouquet.

We named the ministry "Flowers for the Chosen," and I've had some of my friends with floral businesses help to provide flowers for it as well. I still serve today, by request. Widows can be hard to track down, as they sometimes make decisions and moves without telling anyone. But we do our best to make sure they all have a bouquet on their birthday.

Day to day (as you get older and have a few more doctors), I started bringing a bouquet of flowers to receptionists and nurses at the doctors office. No matter how difficult their situation, the gesture always puts smiles on their faces. As I do this, I remember this quote from an anonymous author: "I would rather have one little rose from the garden of a friend, than to have the choicest flowers when my stay on earth must end." Those who receive my roses feel seen and loved.

In 2018, I started another ministry: weddings.

Many young people in the church struggle to afford wedding flowers. I talked to the church leadership and volunteered to do flowers for their weddings. I'd never done a professional bouquet, so I took classes to learn how to make arrangements, bouquets, and boutonnieres. From then on, I did flowers anytime someone requested help for a wedding. I listened to the couples' themes, put the arrangements together, and partnered with friends in downtown Nashville for discounted and free flowers. People give money towards this ministry, and it is hard work. I'm not (and have never been) in the floral business ... but two or three times per year, I provide flowers for weddings like a floral company would!

Weddings are expensive, and young people in the church don't always have the money to purchase full floral arrangements for their ceremony. I'm happy to provide a service that saves them money and give them an extra spark of beauty on their special day. I remember what it was like to be young and married ... and needing to save every dollar we could!

Without John Curtis' influence, I never would have thought about all these ways to minister to people. Think about that, as you cultivate your rose garden. How many people around you could benefit from the flowers you grow? Even if it's just stopping in to say hello to a neighbor, or thanking your child's teacher for their hard work with a beautiful bouquet. Men, women, and children alike love a vase of flowers. It's hard to go wrong with them. It's a pathway to an instant smile, and just the thing to help them feel more relaxed.

People love roses because they connect the past and the present. You can reach people with your rose garden, just like I have. And now is the time to get started.

In the next chapter, we'll talk about some ways to do that.

Bouquets for local retirement communities and our church ministry

Putting together bouquets to give away

A garden gala for the residents of Park Place Retirement Community. My annual Master Gardener project

Zinnias and hydrangeas make great bouquet companion flowers for roses

My Garden at Gadwall Abbey

Part 3

Chapter Five –

Where Should You Start?

By now I hope you're excited at the idea of growing your own roses and building connection with people through them. At this point, people usually ask, "Ron, if I want to grow roses, where do I start?"

There isn't an "easy" answer to that question, but I'll do my best to break it down. You see, you have to accept in your own mind that roses are a challenge to grow. This is no easy hobby, and it will keep you humble. My dad used to tell me, "There is no such thing as a no-maintenance plant." Even silk and plastic plants need a good dusting! You can't start a hobby like this and think it won't require both your time and effort to succeed.

Having said that, I've outlined a step-by-step process to help you start your own garden. This list comes from 30+ years of growing roses. I follow this process anytime I start a garden of my own, or help another person start theirs. It's the process I teach in several workshops, but there's a catch: if you do it all by yourself, this program is hit-or-miss. What you really need are fellow rosarians in your corner. They'll help you more than any book or how-to guide. Doing roses without help and guidance is how most people fail.

If you start working with other rosarians, however, this next chapter has what you need, how to get started, and which roses are available for your personal rose garden.

The Step-By-Step Guide

When I moved to my current residence, I had the opportunity to take my previous rose garden with me. I had developed that garden for 19 years, and I was proud of it.

As we went through the process of selling the house, I ended up putting a sign in the yard that said, "Garden negotiable with the seller." Our real estate agent was having a tough time selling the house. When people walked by they saw all the work that went into that garden, instead of its beauty, and all they could think was, "I'm not going to be able to keep that garden looking like it does." Eventually, God took pity on me and sent me a buyer who gardened organic vegetables.

The buyer asked to keep about 50% of the garden on the condition that I would come back next spring and give her two lessons on growing roses. We agreed that I would move the half of the garden I wanted to keep. That way, she could use the soil left to grow her vegetables. I came back the next year, and gave her those two lessons. She soaked them up like a sponge!

As for picking out the roses I wanted, I got the opportunity to pick out, tag, pot, and take 30+ rose bushes from that garden. She even let me bring my garden art and fountains! I carefully transplanted everything into my new garden at a darling little corner house which gave the public a full view of all those precious flowers. Currently, I maintain 150+ roses at the time of writing, in 2023. I built all my own hardscapes and amended every bit of the harsh, clay-filled Tennessee soil. After eight years, this garden has become a highly social and interactive place. One day while working, I had 25 cars honk as they passed by!

I've restarted my own garden several times, not to mention all the times I've restored and created gardens for other venues. These sanctuaries of beauty give you the opportunity to be visible, social, and generous with neighbors and strangers. Even my non-gardening wife joins us outside when we have an open garden. The beauty draws people in. And because I have dedicated my life to helping others develop gardens of their own, I want to offer you a step by step process I follow anytime I get a garden started.

Transferring a portion of the garden at my old home when we moved in 2013

#1 Selecting Your Roses

When it comes to selecting roses, the primary resource I recommend is the *American Rose Society Handbook For Selecting Roses*. In this handbook, we rate roses from zero to ten. In reality, there is no "zero" and no "ten," but anything from 7-9 is the best rating, signifying that the roses are easier to grow. Personally, I find these ratings highly accurate. For my gardening, I stay within the 7-9 range. There's no sense making things difficult for myself. I like roses that are easy to grow, and grow well in my area.

If you find a rose you like, look it up in this book. Take it with you on your next shopping trip to the nursery. It'll tell you everything about your rose. Along with the rating, the book will detail how disease-resistant it is, how it produces flowers, and review its durability, size, and height. Too many times I've seen a new gardener pick out a rose just because they like the name of it or how it looks. But then, as they struggle to maintain the plant, they later find out it's rated below a 7 in the *American Rose Society Handbook For Selecting Roses*—a very difficult rose to grow!

Keep your environment in mind when picking roses. Different conditions exist at different elevations and climates. You can't grow any and every rose available. Instead, you should grow the roses that do well in your environmental zone. For example, here in Nashville, I'm in Zone Seven. My roses would not grow well in a place like Wisconsin. If you keep your environment in mind you'll have more success.

The American Rose Society Handbook for Selecting Roses. You can order them online at ars.com

When people select their roses, I often get the question, "Ron, what is *your* favorite rose?"

There is a common saying in the Rose Society I wholeheartedly agree with: "My favorite rose is the one that's blooming today!" I have a favorite rose for every rose type (each type has several species of roses included), but there are a few roses that always grow, and I always recommend. The first three I can think of are Mister Lincoln, Double Delight, and the Peace Rose. They were the first three roses John Curtis helped me pick out for my original rose garden, and they got me hooked. They are all Hybrid Teas, a rose type with several species of roses commonly used in the floral business. I still grow them in my garden today.

My first Double Delight rose, from the original K-Mart roses Mr. Curtis helped me grow

My original Mister Lincoln

My original Peace rose

If you want the types of rose I recommend for beginners, try Mister Lincoln. They have a beautiful aroma and a nice big bloom. They are highly rated Hybrid Tea.

Another great beginner rose is Quietness. This is a highly rated shrub rose - I've turned many people onto them. Admittedly, they plant it with some doubt. The initial shrub, after all, is a tiny cutting. But one year later, when it grows into its own, they call to tell me how much they love Quietness roses. They have a big bloom compared to other shrub roses, and they're very easy to maintain. In my opinion, every rose garden needs Quietness roses.

Quietness roses are wonderful for beginners. They're shrubs that look like hybrid teas, but they're lower-maintenance

Before you start picking the rose you want to cultivate, you ought to discover the different types available to you. Every type listed has several species grouped within and includes different colors and sizes. Studying these variations will help you decide how you want to lay out your garden and narrow your search.

Old Garden Roses

All the roses we have today come from their ancestors - old garden roses - which have grown for hundreds of years. Modern hybridizers have carefully cultivated them for breeding, to create the roses we see today. Old Garden roses are hearty plants. They're disease-resistant, carefree and come in many forms such as shrubs and climbers. Most have a strong fragrance—something people love in a rose garden. You can also get multiple bloom cycles out of them if you deadhead and re-fertilize properly.

Old Gardens have a rich history. To be classified as an Old Garden rose, the species must have existed before the year 1867 - which means these roses existed on estates, castles, manors in the time before Reconstruction. They have served as symbols of beauty for the Queen's Tea, and hosted our Founding Fathers as they framed our nation.

Even though these roses were cultivated years ago, many of them still grow and bloom every year. A rose by the name of Old Blush is an example of a species within the Old Garden Rose type. It's a beautiful rose to grow, existing as far back as 1751! They are a staple in my garden. If you went into any antebellum home in the South, you would likely find this rose in their garden as well.

The Old Blush was hybritized in the mid-Eighteenth Century, and was very common among Antebellum homes in the South

Hybrid Teas

Hybrid Teas make up a large portion of the floral industry. As you walk into a flower shop, they stand out as a "perfect" flower, often coming in the form of the single, long-stemmed roses in vases and bouquets. They come in many colors, shapes, and sizes, and most of them are very fragrant. They can have multiple bloom cycles with the correct care. You can deadhead them and they will bloom again within 3-4 weeks. They do require a little more maintenance on fertilization, spraying and watering, but it pays off. In my garden in Zone Seven, they are some of the top-producing roses. I usually get 3-4 bloom cycles each season out of each plant! They can give you a plethora of roses, and the roses they produce are the type people love to receive as gifts, or use in weddings.

The Crescendo was named after the Nashville Symphony. It's one of my favorite hybrid teas

Grandifloras

These are similar to Hybrid teas in color and shape, but they grow taller than Hybrid Teas. In fact, they can get up to six feet tall! They don't have much fragrance, but are quite pretty and can grow in both bush and tree form. I sometimes use them to get color higher up in my garden.

Anna's Promise roses grow at least six feet tall, and they're named for Anna Bates from the Downtown Abbey PBS series

Floribunda

Much like the Grandifloras, the Floribunda can also grow anywhere from 2-6 feet tall. But, they are more common in landscaping due to how much they bloom. Not only do they have several blooms per bloom cycle, but they'll give you even more bloom cycles with deadheading. On top of that, they have great fragrance and are very durable. In my own garden I grow the Julia Child, a species of Floribunda. People who visit love to look at them and smell their fragrance.

Julia Child roses are named for the famous TV chef. They're bright yellow with an amazing fragrance

Iceberg plants grow white, burgundy or pink roses. You can graft them together to create this multi-colored effect

Polyantha

While smaller flowers and blooms are common with polyantha roses, they are still a vibrant rose with a variety of colors. Developed in the early 1900s, I use them in my personal garden. One species I grow in particular is the Marie Pavie, because it does so well in a container.

Developed in the early 1900s, Marie Pavie roses grow well either in containers or in the ground, and require very little maintenance

Modern Shrub

This rose type contains Quietness, the species I mentioned earlier. Garden centers don't commonly carry this one; you'll likely have to ask them to order it for you. It's one of my favorites because it looks like a Floribunda or a Hybrid Tea, but it has a repetitive bloom and is very low-maintenance. You can grow these roses all the way up in Zone Four, close to Canada!

Miracle on the Hudson roses are modern shrubs named after 'The Miracle on the Hudson,' when pilot Chesley Sullenberger landed a civilian airliner on the Hudson River

Miniature

Though these roses grow on large bushes, the flowers themselves are typically small. Being less than three feet tall, this quaint rose has plenty of varieties and colors. They're hardy and cold resistant. If you are just starting out with limited garden space, a miniature may be right for you. They do well in pots and show up frequently at rose shows. My favorite miniature rose is the Daddy Frank, due to its deep red color and Hybrid Tea appearance. It's a great show rose!

My friend Robby Tucker hybridized the Daddy Frank rose. His uncle was called 'Daddy Frank,' and I also called my father-in-law 'Daddy Frank'

Miniflora

Slightly larger than the miniature, the Miniflora's bloom often measures three inches across. The Princess Katelyn is a great rose species here. In fact, a friend of mine hybridized this rose. Between that, and the fact that my own daughter's name is Katelyn, I enjoy growing it in my garden.

My friend, the late Richard Anthony, hybridized the Princess Katelyn rose. Both his niece and my daughter shared the name 'Katelyn'

Climbers (Trainers)

Many mistake climbing roses for vines, when in fact they are called "trainers." This means they are tied off on a wall, trellis, pergola or fence, so the grower can train the plant to bend and twist in certain ways. They can be put on trellises, arbors, pergolas, and buildings. A gardener can shape their long, pliable canes. If you deadhead, they will bloom repeatedly and offer a good amount of color up high. The Jeanne Lajoie climbing miniature is highly rated in the *American Rose Society Handbook For Selecting Roses* at a Nine, and does well anywhere you put it. When it blooms, it has more flowers than other climbers in comparison.

America hybrid teas and Jeanne Lajoie miniatures are among my favorite climber roses

New Dawn roses were hybridized in1930. They were the first roses I ever saw in Mam Maw Powell's garden as a child

Ground Cover Roses

These roses stick close to the ground and usually don't get much more than three feet tall. They are used in landscaping, require low maintenance, and serve as a pretty way to cover a large area. They grow about four feet wide. Pink Splash is a pretty species of ground cover rose, often referred to as "flower carpet."

Standard (Tree Roses)

These roses get grafted up high and grow on an elongated stem, giving them the look of a tree with a single stem shooting up and branching out into several branches of roses at the top. They grow 2 to 5 feet tall and different colors of roses can be grafted into a single tree. However, they do not like the cold. If you live in a zone with a cold winter, you'll likely have to bring them into a garden room or cover them to keep them from freezing.

Floribundas can also be standard tree roses, especially when they're grafted together

Species Roses (Wild Roses)

The species type, or "wild roses" as they are often called, are just like their name sounds: they can be found in the wild, and are immensely hearty. If you have wild roses and you want to grow them, they do well with a cutting.

A particular species rose called the Peggy Martin (or Katrina Rose) is found close to New Orleans. This rose was grown by a specific family over several generations and blooms a gorgeous neon pink. They were thought to be completely lost when Hurricane Katrina came through, but due to their hearty nature, they began to grow again a few weeks later. Reluctant to lose such a gorgeous species, the family decided to offer cuttings, so others could grow them as well. I was lucky enough to get some of the first cuttings! Today this rose still grows in my garden, cascading over my fence. I get many compliments on them!

A Peggy Martin in full bloom.
These roses survived Hurricane Katrina in 2005

Which type stands out to you? Make sure it matches your location and has a high rating. Now that you know more about the roses you can choose from, and have an idea of what you want, let's talk about location.

#2 Choose Your Location

Remember how I said that people experience hardship in their garden because they plant in the wrong location? Roses don't live well under northern exposure. They need about 4-6 hours or more of sunlight each day, and they should be planted facing east, south, or west. Also, keep in mind the size of the rose you want to grow. You need one space if you grow Miniatures, and another if you grow Grandifloras. The space you have available should be big enough to comfortably encompass the rose bushes you're planting.

If the location you pick is ideal for a raised bed, I recommend building one. Not only can you get more drainage out of a raised bed (which is good for roses because they don't like wet feet), but they are also easier to maintain. It's easier to install a drip water system within a raised bed. Although you can get good results planting at ground level, a raised bed offers more control of the soil.

When considering a raised bed, remember - you can use any building material. Wood ties, stacked stone, modular block, brick and concrete walls, and composite lumber all work. There is no "right" or "wrong" way to build a raised bed. The materials only need to hold your soil in place so it doesn't wash away.

#3 Planting

You can accomplish planting a few ways depending on how you purchase your roses.

At rose growing farms, mostly in California, Arizona, and Texas, they traditionally harvest roses and prepare them for shipping in two different ways. Some get placed in three-gallon containers. These are known as "container" roses. Others are classified as "bare root" roses, where the farmer clips back the top of the plant and pulls the entire plant out of the dirt - including the root. You can also order cuttings. They will come in a small container. Most old garden roses,shrubs and miniatures are sold as cuttings and are on there own root. These are very hardy and do good in most zones. They are called own root roses.

The most common way roses come to market is as container roses. I recommend you purchase them at a nursery, because a box store rose is likely going to be a lower-rated rose. Container roses are rated with a grading. If you pay attention to this grading it'll help you pick out a high quality rose. Look for a "number one" grading. This means the rose has three or more canes at the base of the plant. Anything less is not a number one grade. In Zone Seven where I live, the best time to plant these is the middle to end of April.

Potted Lynn Anderson roses at Woodlawn Cemetery in Nashville, where country singer Lynn Anderson was buried

My friend Jeff Smith, owner of S&W Greenhouse, who pots for Certified, Jackson/Perkins and Weeks Nurseries

How bare root roses look before they're planted

If you're ever unsure when to plant a rose, look at its species on the American Rose Society website, ARS.org, or your local rose society website.

When I get a container rose, the first thing I do before I transfer it into my garden is deadhead the blooms. I remember gathering a group of people around once to show them how I transferred a potted plant to my garden. The minute I started cutting off blooms, people gasped in surprise. One lady asked me, "Why are you cutting those off?" I understood her question; many people purchase roses based on the flowers they see growing in the nursery. To cut them off feels counterintuitive ... but I recommend you deadhead your roses before you transfer them into your garden. It sends all of the plant's energy to the roots and help it establish itself quickly. The blooms will come later.

If you purchase a bare root rose instead of a container rose, the process looks a bit different.

I like my bare root roses to be 50/50. This means 50% of the plant is cane and 50% is root. It's a tradeoff: bare root roses are cheaper than container roses, but more hands-on when it comes to planting. When I prepare to plant bare root roses in the dirt, I soak them in water for 24 hours. John Curtis taught me a little trick: in that water, add a few drops of bleach into a five gallon bucket where all your roses are soaking. This is sure to kill any kind of disease that may come from their original location in the growing fields.

After I soak them, I plant them in a pot first, before they go in my garden. That way I have more control of the conditions they grow in. The roses seem to establish themselves a bit quicker. There's no need to worry about outside conditions if I cultivate their root system in my garden house.

When the time comes to plant either a bare root or container rose, you want to put them into the soil at ground level. Afterwards, you provide them with some extra nutrients to get started. In colder zones, plant them a few inches below ground level.

Start by checking the pH levels of the soil. In my garden, the levels are usually a little low, so I'll add a cup of lime around the base of the plant. Remember, for roses the pH level needs to be between 6.0 and 6.5. If your pH level is high, you can add a cup of sulfur instead of lime.

Once the pH is fixed, add some organic matter for fertilizer. This could be plant or animal matter, like compost or bone meal. Then give the plant a nice soak to make sure all the added nutrients get into the root system.

I also add a layer of mulch on top. Mulch lowers weeds, keeps the soil moist, and creates an attractive base in any garden. It comes in several different options and colors. Your neighborhood nursery should have a few good options, but you'll need to look at your home and decide on the best color for your yard.

Growing Roses In Containers

Roxanne Veranda roses in a container

I recommend the following container sizes:(or larger)

- Miniatures and Minifloras: 5-10 gallons(or larger)

- Hybrid Teas and Larger Roses: 20-25 gallons(or larger)

Make sure you use light-colored, plastic containers. Do not use black containers. Drainage is very important for roses; be sure to drill extra holes in the bottom of your container. An inch or two of gravel in the bottom of the container will help with drainage.

Plant your roses in a good potting soil with moisture control. Use liquid fertilizer to fertilize your container rose bushes, every 10-14 days. My favorite brands for this are MiracleGro or Beaty's Fertilizer's Organic Easy Feed. Just add one tablespoon per gallon of water.

Correct your pH levels the same way you would with regular roses you plant in the ground, with levels between 6.0 to 6.5. Lime will raise your pH level, and sulfur will bring it down. Container-grown roses need watering more often, especially when it's hot. In the hot seasons you should water them daily.

Special Note: Here are the kind of roses that grow good in containers:

- Miniature
- Miniflora
- Shrub
- Floribunda
- Some Hybrid Teas
- Some (smaller) Old Garden roses

If you like to move your roses around the garden a couple of times per year, you can add casters or wheels on the bottoms of the containers. It's also a good idea to maintain the containers 2-3 times per year - apply one tablespoon of Clearex Salt Leaching Solution per gallon of water. First, water the pots, and then pour one gallon around the base of the bush. This helps prevent salt buildup, which makes it easier for fertilizer to get into the bush.

#4 Develop A Maintenance Schedule

After you've planted your roses, you need a maintenance schedule. If you try to maintain your roses without a schedule, you will forget certain steps to achieve those beautiful, desirable blooms.

Here I will cover the four key parts of a good maintenance schedule: watering, fertilization, spraying and pruning.

a. Watering

Roses require a lot of water. You can't depend on rainfall to sustain them, even in wet climates. I recommend a watering schedule based on the temperature of your zone. If your roses are planted in pots you'll need to water them every day, because they will dry faster than roses in the ground.

- 50-60's - water every 3 days
- 60-80s - water every 2 days
- 90+ - water every day

You can water your roses several different ways. Personally, I prefer a drip water system placed directly at the base of the plant. That way, I don't waste water. Additionally, I can set them up on a timer. However, some people like to use a soaker hose, where you run a hose around the plants with water dripping from various pores in the hose. Soaker hoses can also be used with timers.

If you have a small rose garden (about 2-3 roses), or are just starting out, I recommend watering by hand using a hose. Make sure it isn't overhead water—you don't want to get any water on the leaves. Place the hose at the base of each plant. Hand watering will allow you to get closer to your plants and you'll be quicker to catch any changes that might need your attention.

But whatever watering method you use, make sure you water deeply. The ground should be soaked a few inches in depth once you're done. Additionally, if you go to water but the ground is still moist, go ahead and skip watering for that day.

b. Fertilization

Make a schedule for when to fertilize your garden.

Personally, I fertilize three times a year - in the spring, when my garden first wakes up from winter; after the first bloom cycle in the middle of June; and after the second bloom cycle in August. That is my last fertilization of the year, because it's not good to fertilize right before winter. Here are the specifics:

- First application: End of March to mid-April

    - 2-3 cups organic or Beaty Fertilizer (Magic Mills Mix) around each rose bush

    - 1 cup Osmocote 14-14-14 slow release granular fertilizer

- Second application: Beginning-to-mid June

- Same as above, but with only ½ cup of Osmocote
- Third application: end of August to first of September
  - Same as 2nd application

Remember - this is for Zone Seven, where I live. The times and dates will vary through different time zones and climates.

When I fertilize, I also check the pH levels of the soil and make any necessary adjustments. If they're low, I'll add ½ a cup to 1 cup of Dolomitic lime (garden lime). If they're high, I'll add ½ a cup to 1 cup of sulfur. (For miniature roses, use only half of these amounts).

I use a combination of organic fertilizer and synthetic fertilizer. For my organic fertilizer, I use alfalfa meal, bone meal, worm castings and Mills Mix, made by Beaty Fertilizer. For synthetic, I use granular fertilizer - Bloomkote (Beaty Fertilizer) or 14-14-14 Osmocote. Be sure to cover up fertilizers after you apply them, and give them plenty of water.

Between these fertilization cycles, I also use a liquid fertilizer called Easy Feed. When using this product, you need to water your plant first, then put the liquid around it, and do not water again immediately after. If you don't water the plant first, your liquid fertilizer will run away from the plant. And if you water after, you'll dilute the fertilizer.

That's how I do it. Other rosarians may have different fertilization programs to get to that perfect rose.

Bloomkote, Mills Mix and Easy Feed by Beaty Fertilizer. My preferred brand

c. Pruning

Once your fertilization schedule is set, you need to develop a pruning schedule. Pruning a rose plant is like grooming a dog - a good habit to maintain the health of your garden. Though most pruning happens in the spring—where you cut back the dead from your roses so new growth can start—you'll also continue to deadhead during the entire season.

First, let's talk about spring pruning. Make sure you have good rose gloves on! As the old song goes, every rose has its thorns! You'll also need a good pair of sharp pruners. To ensure disease doesn't spread as you use them, I keep a spray bottle of rubbing alcohol handy. I spray alcohol on the pruners in between each plant.

Begin at the top of the bush and work your way down. The first cuts you make will feel a bit radical. Don't be afraid - you're not "killing the plant" because you cut it way down and it looks small and stumpy afterwards. You're not hurting it; the goal of these first cuts is to lower and shape the bush, and get old or dead branches out of the way. Browned or browning cane should be cut. Even if the cane is only half brown, they're unlikely to produce a flower. This trimming also includes any branch smaller than a number two pencil. Small branches won't produce many roses, so removing them will allow the plant to focus its energy on the stronger canes. The end goal is to have the thickest green canes remaining.

The more you prune, the more natural it will feel. People see me pruning and feel intimidated by how fast I move, and how quickly I can identify a dying cane from a healthy one. But this is a skill that took time to develop—and it's one you'll learn, if you do enough of it consistently.

Once you've finished these first cuts, you'll need to be more precise about the pruning. Check for bud eyes. These are the beginnings of a new branch. You'll likely find several on any one cane, and it will become the next area in the cane where the shoot grows. Place your pruning shears right above the bud eye and cut at a 45 degree angle. In the second round of pruning, follow the same principle as you work through the plant. You need good air circulation through the bush so make sure you have plenty of space between the canes. If you do this right, all the canes you leave should produce flowers.

After the initial pruning, the rest of the year's pruning will consist of deadheading your roses. The goal of deadheading is to remove wilting flowers and encourage new growth. If you don't deadhead your flowers, the rose bush will go to seed and you won't get anymore blooms out of that bush. When you identify a wilting or spent flower, or you cut one to bring into the house, cut all Hybrid tea roses just above a five leaf. All other spent blooms can be deadheaded at any location on the bush. That way, you encourage new growth from the bush.

Remember, there is no such thing as "bad pruning," unless it is *no pruning at all*. It's a skill that takes practice, but I promise you'll get better the more you do it.

Before pruning

After pruning

Special Note: Keep the tetanus shots up.

#5 Preventing Disease and Insects

Diseases

Special Note: <u>Use preventatives</u>. The easiest problem to solve is the one you don't have in the first place.

When growing roses, the number one disease you will fight in most parts of the country is black spot. This disease can creep up on your roses if they experience too much moisture combined with high temperatures. But don't worry if you begin to see these little black spots on your leaves. There is a solution.

I like to use Fungicides, Banner Maxx and Honor Guard (or Propiconazole) as preventatives for black spots (⅓ to ⅔ teaspoons per gallon of water). They are easy to use and only require you to spray down your roses with them every 15 days (or two times a month). If you still get them, there is a great product that takes them out quickly: Manzate. Spray it on, and watch the black spots fade. When you do this, be sure to scoop up any fallen leaves around the plant, so you can prevent disease from transferring to other rose bushes in your garden. Follow the directions on all fungicides. (MIX: one tablespoon per gallon of water)

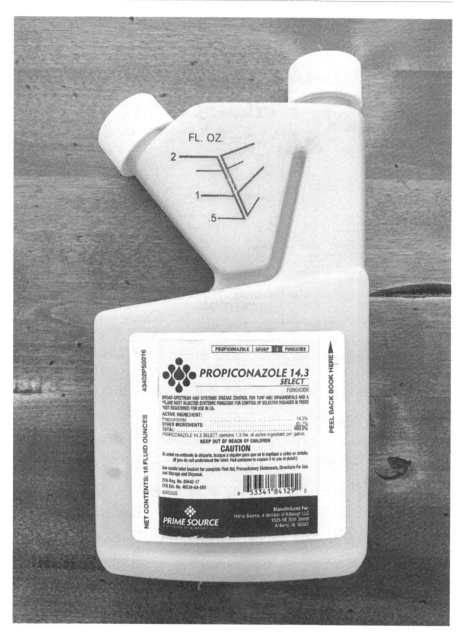

Propiconazole - a preventative fungicide to keep black spots away

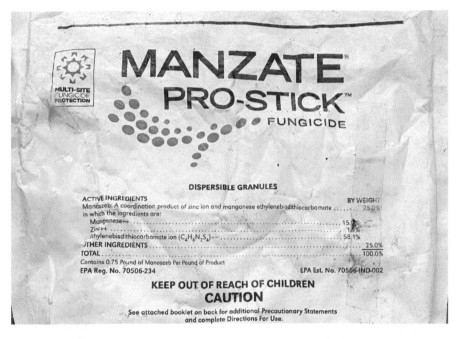

Manzate - the best fungicide for getting rid of black spots

Another common disease is mildew. Both of the preventative sprays I just mentioned will help you avoid this disease, which appears as a white powdery substance on the leaves. If it does plague your roses, remove all infected leaves and dispose of them. If you don't want to spray your roses, there's a group of roses that have been tested without a spray program, and they're very hardy. This group is called the "Earth Kind Roses." You can find a list of them on the internet. They're not maintenance-free, of course, but they do well in most zones.

Insects

In Zone Seven, Japanese beetles come every year. Unfortunately, they like to munch on the petals of your flowers.

A product called Merit 75 WP will keep them under control (⅛ teaspoon per gallon of water). Thrips are bugs that get inside your bloom and destroy the center. I use a product called Conserve, and spray the buds directly with it to keep them from destroying the bud (1 tablespoon per gallon of water). And if you have roses up against a wall, you might have to deal with spider mites. Luckily, spider mites don't need a chemical or pesticide; you can wash them off your plant with a hose. Remember to do this in the early morning, so your roses have plenty of time for leaves to dry. Follow the directions on all insect products.

(Organic fundigicides and insecticides can also be used ,but you will have to spray more often.)

Japanese beetles are the most common pests for rosarians

Conserve is excellent for keeping thrips away from your roses

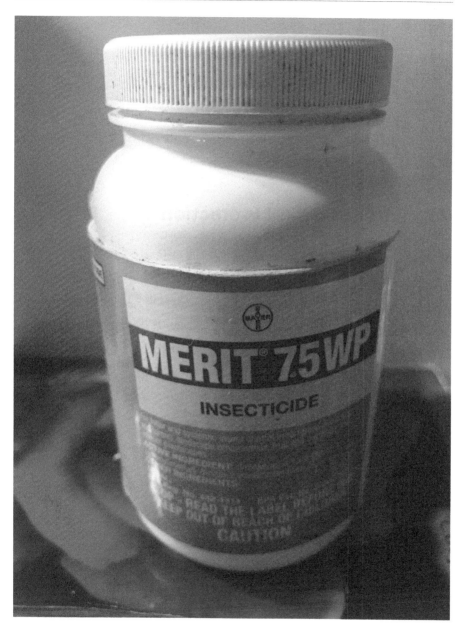

I use Merit to deter Japanese beetles and other insects

If you follow these steps, you should have the beginnings of a successful rose garden. While there will be other challenges to crop up and surprise you, these are the steps I follow any time I focus on building and maintaining a new garden. If you follow them and consult other rosarians in your area, you'll find your way to a beautiful rose garden in your yard.

Special Note: Keep a garden calendar to track the maintenance on your roses.

#6 Winter Care and Protection

Winter protection varies, depending on the growing zone. Here in Zone Seven, I mound around all my grafted roses 12 to 14 inches high with mulch, to protect the bud union (where it is grafted to root stock). If this part freezes, it'll kill the rose bush. You want to maintain the same temperature around the grafted areas. All own-root roses like Miniatures, Old Garden Roses,Shrubs and others are hardy, and require little protection.

I put 3-4 inches of mulch around each plant. Tree roses are grafted up high on the bush, and need to be stored in a garden room or garage. The same goes for roses planted in containers. Check with your local rose society for growing zone recommendations to protect your roses and winterize your garden. Also, be sure to plant roses that do well in your zone.

My garden under a full winter's snow

A mound of brown mulch will protect the roots and the base of the plant from snow and frost

St. Patrick roses are very sensitive to cold, so I build a plastic wire collar and fill it with mulch to keep their roots warm

Special Note: Keep roses healthy during growing season, and they will be stronger during the wintertime. Roses have an immune system like people do, so make sure your roses have good ones!

Chapter Six –

More Than A Hobby

Now that you know how to develop your garden, I advise you to pay it forward. In the words of John Curtis, "Go show someone else what you have learned!"

Not only does rose growing keep you humble, but you also have to learn that they are all a little different—which means you, as the gardener, have to handle each one differently. Everytime you think you've got it figured out, something changes. But if you stick to it, you might start to notice how growing roses is like dealing with people. Each one's a little different, but you can find ways to help them, and you can bet God is pleased with you when you're helping His other children.

Growing Roses Is Like Raising Kids

If you're blessed with kids, you likely feel the same way. When my own children were young, we constantly dealt with and worked through new challenges. Growth spurts, new emotions, new teachers and classes, and new social settings to understand. All these things keep parents and children on their toes. If you have more than one child, you know each one is unique. They respond differently to the discipline and encouragement you offer, so you handle them differently. As a parent, you have to be fluid and flexible, with a level head to guide your children through each stage of development. Kids remember the times you spend with them, and roses will respond to time spent and how you care for them also.

I can look back over 30 years of gardening and identify a stressful part of *every single* season. There were always times when I needed to be flexible and find solutions for a struggling bush in the garden. Even with my experience, there will never be a "perfect" season where nothing goes wrong.

One time, we had a drought in our area. The roses were stressed and unhappy with the water I gave them. Like a lot of parents with their teenagers, I was tempted to blame the roses, or the lack of rain—but that wasn't going to change the results. So, I stayed on course with my maintenance cycle. While doing so, I paid special attention to fertilization, pruning, and deadheading. During this time, when I couldn't water them as much as I liked, I stayed in tune with them - even when it was stressful for me. With proper care and maintenance, the rose garden still had a successful season, even with less water than they liked. I addressed the problem head on and tried several different solutions, until I found the ones that worked.

Hard times catch new gardeners by surprise and tempt them to feel like they are "failing" because their garden is struggling. Every new gardener wants to win right away, and who doesn't prefer winning to losing? But what makes you successful is the inner strength to be an "effective loser" - taking failure in stride, and learning from it. Let's use sports, for example. It's easy to hoop and holler when your team wins, but losing hurts us to the core. Pride and ego take a blow. And very few people know how to handle loss in the right way.

With roses, "losses" come in many forms. It's usually insects, black spots, mold, mildew, drought, extreme cold, wind and other environmental influences. How you deal with adversity in your garden determines the outcome; if you can look at problems or losses in your garden as learning opportunities, you'll do just fine. There is always one more idea you haven't tried yet, and plenty of people like me who love to help others improve. I believe every novice rose grower should take this into account before they start. It's less of a shock or surprise that way, when you encounter the challenging side of growing.

When things get tough, remember this quote from Abraham Lincoln. "We can complain because rose bushes have thorns, or rejoice because thorn bushes have roses." Another great quote by an anonymous author says, "When life throws thorns, hunt for roses."

Many people mistakenly hope to avoid difficulties by simply placing their roses in ideal growing conditions. In reality, when you grow *anything* in the ground, you have to accept that you can only control a small portion of the plant's environment. It's nice to get ideal circumstances, but you're much more likely to find ones that are "less than ideal." No matter where you plant or how well you follow your maintenance schedule, problems will arise.

John Curtis once said, "Only God can grow roses. Rosarians are mere conduits of health."

That's true of a lot of things people do, and it's especially true in gardening. We're taking plants out of their natural environments and putting them in our yards and gardens. Because of this, we must become conduits of the plant's health and happiness. They're our responsibility.

That means *you* have to adjust to the environment - more than the plant does. It's a challenge when you're growing things. You might spend a lot of time wondering why the plants don't adapt, when the real question is, "How adaptable are *you*?" Not the roses, soil, or fertilizer - you! The true success story is when *you* become adaptable, and can keep a level head as you deal with issues in your garden.

Roses should be therapeutic and life-giving. Moving through challenges with them is part of the process, and it's a process of love. If you stop for a moment and think about anything else that's therapeutic or life-giving ... whatever it might be, it doesn't just "happen." A loving grandparent, a skilled therapist, an affirming mentor and even a relaxing time in the spa all take the same thing: *lots of work*, and learning to do things better today than you did yesterday.

For me, during the COVID-19 pandemic, my rose garden meant I had somewhere to go to be outdoors. Though the world was in chaos around me, my rose garden still needed my attention. I fell into the routine of my maintenance schedule while others were bogged down with depression and fear. Instead of being locked in my home, I was outside *literally* smelling the roses!

I urge you to remember - though rose growing will test you, it's a great outlet to find simplicity and balance. As long as you understand problems in your rose garden are normal (even for master rosarians), you'll find joy and meaning in this work.

Mentorship Makes A Difference

With everything I've achieved in the rose world, I'm at my happiest when I'm teaching others. Mentoring has changed my life. John was right to push me on the importance of teaching someone else. I now understand where his joy came from, much better than I used to. He drew deep satisfaction from sharing his passion with others.

As I followed in his footsteps, it led me to mentoring a man by the name of John Wendler, my dear friend, who wrote the foreword of this book. After retiring as National Marketing Director for the Tractor Supply company, we met when he decided to try his hand at growing roses. He came to the

Nashville Rose Society meeting. The first time we spoke he said, "I don't know a thing about roses."

I knew what to say - the same words John Curtis said to me decades earlier: "Don't worry, I'll teach you."

Together we came up with a plan for his first rose garden. It took me back to my first moments with my mentor and those K-Mart rose bushes. As we picked out the roses, prepared the soil, and added a water system, I had flashbacks to the time when I was the student, not the teacher. In return for my help, John Wendler helped us at the Nashville Rose Society tackle our marketing (which none of us knew much about) and became an active member.

Today he grows over 70 roses and is a consulting rosarian. He worked hard, learned a lot, and developed a fulfilling passion to help others. You will too.

After 10 years, you can be recognized as an ARS master consulting rosarian as well. You can become part of a network that grows roses together and lifts each other up. Many people join for more than the roses. They join for the opportunity to teach others and learn more themselves. This is why the power of the rose lies in paying it forward. Any person you teach or mentor has the potential to make a significant impact of their own.

One of the last photos taken of Mr. Curtis in his garden

Roses Leave A Lasting Impression

Time passed, and I worked hard to leave a lasting impact on the rosarian world. I finished the project at Belmont. I worked on projects at Belle Air Mansion and the Hermitage. I help to restore private gardens for people who buy new homes, when they don't know how to take care of the roses in their new gardens. I worked on projects for elementary schools, memorials and city properties. By working with roses, I get to impact lives ... thousands of lives.

Every spring, I run workshops. My garden is accessible for people to walk through, as they learn the secrets of caring for roses. Some people see it as they're passing by, and decide to walk through. Others nearing the ends of their lives come hoping to see something beautiful. Still others are new rosarians looking to learn and improve. No matter who comes by, everyone is welcome.

As your roses grow, be on the lookout for occasions to use them. You can leave a lasting impression on the world around you. You can also show your roses at rose shows, Rose Societies, and county and state fairs - great places to see the best of each variety you might want to grow.

A rose tour I gave in 2019 guiding people from 30 states through the Belmont Rose Garden, the Rose Study Garden at Cheekwood and my personal garden

What Do I Do Now?

I started with a handful of K-Mart roses and no idea of how I would care for them. But through mentors, trial and error, community, and ministry, I have become a master rosarian. And you can too.

You don't have to do this alone. No matter where you live, there is likely a Rose Society or a Master Gardener Association near you. You have access to more people who are willing to help than you realize. If you're in my area, come on by and join the Nashville Rose Society. Here, you can attend some of our workshops, meet some great speakers and a community of rosarians willing to help.

Roland A. Brown once said, "I don't know whether nice people tend to grow roses, or growing roses makes people nice." He was right. The people at NRS, as well as most rosarians you'll encounter, are kind people - quick to offer a helping hand and a word of encouragement or advice.

Of course, my garden is always open to visitors as well. If you'd like to schedule a visit, email me at rosetherapy23@gmail.com. I also send out an invitation to my open garden twice a year!

If you're outside Nashville, you can contact me through social media. People send me pictures of problems with their roses and ask for advice. Others send pictures of roses that need pruning and ask me how they should do it. Whenever you get stuck, I'm one quick message away. Find me on Facebook and reach me at NashvilleRoseSociety.org anytime.

If you're part of a larger group looking for a speaker, I'm happy to help. You can invite me to speak at your conference, company event, or garden show. I'll teach you the basics I've mentioned in this book, and give you hands-on experience in cultivating your own roses. I also love to share my knowledge and passions on podcasts, radio, YouTube or TV shows (I'm a regular guest on the RoseChat podcast). I will consider any opportunity to spread the joy of growing and cultivating roses.

I hope this book ignites your passion, and gives you a baseline for where to start with your own rose garden. Remember to minister to people around you, and take others under your wing as you work toward mastery. Share the beauty of your garden with the world. Don't build something beautiful, only to lock people out from experiencing it. Take every opportunity you can to help people learn and find joy. Through your generosity and guidance, you just might change someone's life.

About The Author

Ron is a 3rd generation gardener who loves and enjoys growing roses. He also shares his experience with others who have the same desire to grow champion roses and other plants and to do so successfully. Below are some of his rose growing achievements and skills:

- Master Consulting Rosarian with the American Rose Society

- Member of Nashville Rose Society – 2009 Bronze Medal Winner – Co-President or President for 5 years

- ARS Master Rosarian, ARS Glenda Whitaker Award for Membership

- Consulting Rosarian for Belmont University Adelecia Acklen Rose Garden, Manage the Rose Study Garden at Cheekwood and other public and private gardens

- Master Gardener for Sumner County Master Gardeners of the State of Tennessee

- Marketing Representative for "Holy Cow!" premium soil mix

- Garden speaker with the main topic of Growing and Caring for Roses

- Featured guest on 3 shows of the Volunteer Gardener, a national cable NPT tv program. Can find them on Youtube under the following names: Glorious Garden in a Suburban Lot, Ron Daniels and Types of Roses

- Featured regular guest on Rose Chat Blog Talk Radio Show with the topic being "How to Grow Roses"

Acknowledgements

When a book gets written, many people contribute without ever writing a word.

It's *who they are*, and the things they say and do that sink deep into the memories and heart of the author, that fills me with gratitude to the following people:

To **John Curtis**, my dear departed friend and mentor - I can't thank you enough for introducing me to growing, caring for and sharing roses.

To **Shannon Lane** - you introduced me to John, and encouraged me to listen to him. Simple, small things can have such a huge impact.

To my daughter, **Katelyn Huddleston**, who has always supported me, helped with Power Point presentations and photos, and (of course) with this book, as I've taken my journey with growing roses. I love you!

To my three greatest gardening mentors - **Lester Earl Daniels**, my dad; **Albert Sharron** - my grandfather; and **Mam Maw Powell** - my grandmother. Without them, I wouldn't know the value gardening brought to my life.

To **Todd and Kathy Morrison**. Thank you for encouraging me through all these years. Thanks Kathy for sharing my garden with the public, and helping me get on *Volunteer Gardener* on PBS. You guys are the best at marketing my passion, my garden and my knowledge of roses.

To **Teresa Byington**, my friend and the hostess of the RoseChat Podcast. Thanks for your encouragement and support, and sharing me and my rose garden with the world.

To **John Wendler**, my dear friend and co-leader of the Nashville Rose Society. I'm proud to call you a friend and an American Rose Society Consulting Rosarian.

To **Charles Lott, Sam Jones** and **Jeff Smith** - three great men who influenced me in my journey of growing and caring for roses.

And to **Francine Daniels**, my wife of 55 years, who allowed me to pursue my passion of gardening, growing and caring for roses for 30 years. I love you!

Additional Resources

Nashville Rose Society

American Rose Society

Weeks Roses

Certified Roses

The Antique Rose Emporium

K + M Roses

A Reverence For Roses

High Country Roses

S + W Greenhouse

Beaty Fertilizer

Mills Mix

Holy Cow Soils

Rosemania

References